A SEASON OF GRATITUDE
A DAY AT A TIME
(AKA: A giraffe named Gratitude)

4/2016

DEAR J.J. GARRETT,
YOU ARE SUCH A WONDERFUL
YOUNG PERSON THAT SIGRID AND RON
DALE ASKED ME TO SEND THIS
BOOK AS A GIFT TO YOU FROM
THEIR HEARTS.
WE ALL HOPE YOU USE
AND ENJOY THIS GIFT.

By
Garie Thomas-Bass
GARIE THOMAS-BASS

Illustrated by
KAREEM BLACK

FYI: Another book written by this author is entitled:

<u>Purposeful (Not Random) Acts of Kindness (AKA Beginning Steps for Overcoming Spoiled Brat-a holism)</u>

Note: The author has made a pledge to personally donate 10% of the profits from the sale of this book to The American Society for the Prevention of Cruelty to Animals (ASPCA).

This book is dedicated to ALL of my wonderful family members and friends. I am using author's privilege to give extra special acknowledgement to: our mom, Mrs. Rose Thomas, who made her transition in July 2003. I give gratitude for her every single day;

-my husband, Paul Bass, who is my best friend, an excellent husband, an amazing HVAC engineer, and he helped me with all things computer-related for my book;

-my two sisters, Kertia Black and Bertha Thomas - Kertia is an amazing role model as a super smart medical doctor, someone with unlimited energy, and a very caring person; - Bertha is fantastically wise (EQ and IQ), goal-oriented, and loved by everyone;

-my two brothers, Kirtis Thomas III and Kabin Alan Thomas - Kirtis is a miracle of modern medicine, he has a marvelous mind that creates thousands of inventions, and he is a wonderfully perceptive person who can read people like a book; - Kabin plays the tuba the way Jimi Hendrix played the guitar, he is kind, popular, and he is the creator of the children's character Symphony Sam;

-our Aunt Margueritte Russell (our mom's sister), who is the embodiment of perfect love, intelligence, and patience.

-A very special "Thank You" goes out to my nephew, Kareem Black, an artist and photographer of the highest order, who created the purely beautiful giraffe drawings of Gratitude the Giraffe for my book.

-Thank you so much to Maria Catalfio for guidance about technical rules in book writing.

-Gratitude goes out to the occupational therapy department at the Rehabilitation Institute of Michigan (RIM), especially to Denise (You really helped with the therapy for my elbow, arms, and hand so I could get this done!!!) and Beth (You helped me stay focused on my book's timeline!!!)

Finally, a memorial "thank you" goes to a wonderful soul named Thelma Luster, who started me on the road to sharing five gratitude thoughts a day with "no repeats".
I have an infinite amount of gratitude for every single one of you!!

(Spoiler alert: Water = Prosperity)

Philosophical Question # 1:
How do you see the level of the water in the, always quoted about, water glass?

a) 50% Full?

b) 50% Empty?

c) What water glass????

Philosophical Question # 2:

How do you see the level of the gratitude you offer for any prosperity in your life?

a) 50% Full?

b) 50% Empty?

c) What water glass?????

Philosophical Question # 3:
Is there a connection between the perception of prosperity and the level of gratitude in your life?

This book is here to help find out if this connection can increase a day at a time. Let's begin.

I normally love concrete rules, but in this case, please feel free to write in this book any way that seems most appropriate and beneficial for you. This is YOUR personal space of reflection.

Personally, I was lucky enough to have been part of a wonderful gratitude program. One of the rules that this program insisted on was to write out 5 gratitude thoughts EVERY day with NO REPEATS. The "no repeats" clause was there in order to force me to look at my "every day" with new eyes and to make me see the positives that each day brings. In other words, writing, "I am grateful for air." on Monday and then writing "see Monday" as my entry on Tuesday and maybe even the day after that, would not encouragement me to learn how to reflect on the higher perspectives of life offered to me by the practice of gratitude.

Even though I now understand why, the "no repeats" was important it was definitely the toughest part for me, therefore the creation of this book. Since I did not have a book of prompts like this, I would write out my gratitude thoughts each day on pieces of paper. After a few weeks I found that I could not remember if I had already written gratitude about this or that item. So the writing process became more frustrating rather than reflective. I would say to myself, "There should be a book of prompts to help keep me on track!" Happily this book IS now a reality!

FYI: A quick note about the format in this book: I wrote all 5 gratitude samples (in 2 different ways in fact) on an example page. After that I only give one detailed example for the next 21 pages (3 weeks), and finally I only randomly drop in short examples here and there to hopefully help while still allowing you to make this book totally your own. I'm hoping that the prompts and examples will give you some practice as a gentle starting place until daily gratitude writing becomes an easy and joyful habit.

The following picture is of a giraffe named, of all things, Gratitude. This giraffe will show up throughout the book as a visual reminder or prompt to think from a higher perspective.

I am betting that you are asking the following: "Why did you put the concept of gratitude and the animal, called a giraffe, together??" Well I am glad you asked!

The answer is as follows. It is a fact that giraffes have a wonderful attribute (Height, in their case). This height allows them to see life and access the world from a MUCH higher perspective. This elevated point of view allows them to feed joyfully and abundantly from the best food of fruit and leaves (The giraffe's "supply", so to speak). This higher perspective also allows them the ability to observe much more of the world from the safer venue of that height.

Therefore, looking at giraffes in human terms we would say that they could be considered extremely prosperous! In addition, part of the reason they do so well is because most other animals cannot access the parts of the tree that the giraffes can easily reach because of the gift that the giraffes have of "higher perspective".

One day while observing some giraffes I came to realize that gratitude is the gift that gives humans this type of higher prospective. Gratitude is our way of seeing life from an elevated point of view and accessing a more joyful and abundant world. I have heard it said that how and what we think about life is multiplied. Gratitude for what we have in life brings more positives into our lives to be grateful about each day. In "giraffe terms" it is more abundant food and a safer venue. For humans our abundant lives are manifested in a surprisingly similar way with good food, safety for our family, a comfortable home, etc as our "supply".

Human gratitude perspective is the equivalent version of giraffe height perspective.

That is how my Gratitude the Giraffe idea was born. Thanks to the artistic skill of my nephew, Kareem Black, this beautiful drawing was created as a logo. The giraffe named Gratitude is a reminder that we have the opportunity to see the world from a higher perspective of gratitude in order to access the prosperity that life provides.

Note: Any positive way that you feel comfortable expressing written gratitude is the perfect way for you to use this book! But… just in case you learn the way that I do, and you like to have a starter example then the following is being offered as a concrete sampling of possible ways to get started.

Example: Express 5 gratitude thoughts about your favorite type(s) of fruit.

One way to express gratitude may include listing the attributes of a specific type of fruit like apples…

1) I am extremely grateful for Gala apples.
2) I am grateful that apples are delicious.
3) I am grateful that apples are reasonably priced.
4) I am grateful that apples are readily available all year long.
5) I am grateful that apples are available in a large variety of tastes, types, and colors.

Or you may decide to list five types of fruit that you are grateful for and a reason for each.

1) I am grateful for grapes because they easily fit into my lunch kit.
2) I am grateful for honeydew melon because it can readily be used as a dessert.

3) I am grateful for strawberries because they make great smoothies.
4) I am grateful for bananas because they provide excellent potassium.
5) I am grateful for plums because they are delicious and they provide extra hydration in my day.

We know, for a fact, that you will enjoy this season of gratitude. You will be amazed at the huge difference that "seeing life from a higher perspective" will make in your life. Enjoy your gratitude journey, which begins on the very next page!!!

DAY 1

Express 5 gratitude thoughts about your favorite
type(s) of fruit.

1) _____

_____

_____

2) _____

_____

_____

3) _____

_____

_____

4) _____

_____

_____

5) _____

_____

_____

NOTES:

DAY 2

Express 5 gratitude thoughts for your (living) family members. (I am grateful for my brother, Kirtis, who helps me, figure out my dreams.)

1) _____

_____

_____

2) _____

_____

_____

3) _____

_____

_____

4) _____

_____

_____

5) _____

_____

_____

NOTES:

DAY 3

Express 5 Gratitude thoughts for your (living) friends/associates (I am grateful for my friend, Gawyn Z., who listens to me tell the same story over and over again without complaint.)

1) _____

_____

_____

2) _____

_____

_____

3) _____

_____

_____

4) _____

_____

_____

5) _____

_____

_____

NOTES:

DAY 4

Express 5 Gratitude thoughts for your education or learned skills. (I am grateful for earning my four stationary engineering licenses.)

1) _____

_____

_____

2) _____

_____

_____

3) _____

_____

_____

4) _____

_____

_____

5) _____

_____

_____

NOTES:

DAY 5

Express 5 Gratitude thoughts for your body parts. (I am grateful for my feet carrying me around each day of my entire life.)

1) _____

_____

_____

2) _____

_____

_____

3) _____

_____

_____

4) _____

_____

_____

5) _____

_____

_____

NOTES:

DAY 6

Express 5 Gratitude thoughts for possessions/items in your home. (I am grateful for the PC that I use to write books.)

1) _____

_____

_____

2) _____

_____

_____

3) _____

_____

_____

4) _____

_____

_____

5) _____

_____

_____

NOTES:

DAY 7

Express 5 Gratitude thoughts for essentials in life. (I am grateful for clean air to breathe.)

1) _____

_____

_____

2) _____

_____

_____

3) _____

_____

_____

4) _____

_____

_____

5) _____

_____

_____

NOTES:

DAY 8

Express 5 Gratitude thoughts for favorite books and/or movies. (I am grateful for movies based on the Marvel Universe that allow good to overcome evil.)

1) _____

_____

_____

2) _____

_____

_____

3) _____

_____

_____

4) _____

_____

_____

5) _____

_____

_____

NOTES:

DAY 9

Express 5 Gratitude thoughts for entertainment and/or hobbies. (I am grateful for crochet needles that allow me to make beautiful Afghans.)

1) _____

_____

_____

2) _____

_____

_____

3) _____

_____

_____

4) _____

_____

_____

5) _____

_____

_____

NOTES:

DAY 10

Express 5 Gratitude thoughts for (past or present) pets. (I am grateful for our kitties [named: Data, G, Odo, and Spirit].)

1) _____

_____

_____

2) _____

_____

_____

3) _____

_____

_____

4) _____

_____

_____

5) _____

_____

_____

NOTES:

DAY 11

Express 5 Gratitude thoughts for role models/heroes. (I am grateful for my teacher, Mary Jo Nichols, from University of Detroit Mercy, for making mathematics interesting.)

1) _____

_____

_____

2) _____

_____

_____

3) _____

_____

_____

4) _____

_____

_____

5) _____

_____

_____

NOTES:

DAY 12

Express 5 Gratitude thoughts for (past or present) health and healing. (I am grateful for my feet healing after two full years.)

1) _____

_____

_____

2) _____

_____

_____

3) _____

_____

_____

4) _____

_____

_____

5) _____

_____

_____

NOTES:

DAY 13

Express 5 Gratitude thoughts for modes of transportation. (I am grateful for the first car I ever owned. It was an 8 cylinder 1975 Chevy Nova.)

1) _____

_____

_____

2) _____

_____

_____

3) _____

_____

_____

4) _____

_____

_____

5) _____

_____

_____

NOTES:

DAY 14

Express 5 Gratitude thoughts for all of our senses. (I am grateful for retaining my good hearing even after working around loud equipment for twenty years.)

1) _____

_____

_____

2) _____

_____

_____

3) _____

_____

_____

4) _____

_____

_____

5) _____

_____

_____

NOTES:

DAY 15

Express 5 Gratitude thoughts for unexpected good or acts of kindness. (I am grateful for all of the tall people who help me reach items on upper grocery store shelves.)

1) _____

_____

_____

2) _____

_____

_____

3) _____

_____

_____

4) _____

_____

_____

5) _____

_____

_____

NOTES:

DAY 16

Express 5 Gratitude thoughts for favorite foods. (I am grateful for the vegetarian Botana from Los Galanes in Detroit, Michigan.)

1) _____

_____

_____

2) _____

_____

_____

3) _____

_____

_____

4) _____

_____

_____

5) _____

_____

_____

NOTES:

DAY 17

Express 5 Gratitude thoughts for utilities. (I am grateful for the clean water that is sent to my home each day.)

1) _____

_____

_____

2) _____

_____

_____

3) _____

_____

_____

4) _____

_____

_____

5) _____

_____

_____

NOTES:

DAY 18

Express 5 Gratitude thoughts for communication devices and skills. (I am grateful for my landline telephone because it still worked even when the power was not working for many days in our state.)

1) _____

_____

_____

2) _____

_____

_____

3) _____

_____

_____

4) _____

_____

_____

5) _____

_____

_____

NOTES:

DAY 19

Express 5 Gratitude thoughts for all types of prosperity past and/or present. (I am grateful for winning a contest in 2012 for $2500 (two thousand five hundred dollars) from my job for an idea I submitted.)

1) _____

_____

_____

2) _____

_____

_____

3) _____

_____

_____

4) _____

_____

_____

5) _____

_____

_____

NOTES:

DAY 20

Express 5 Gratitude thoughts for overcoming hardships in life. (I am grateful for being offered early retirement when the school where I was the building engineer for over sixteen years was completely closed and sold.)

1) _____

_____

_____

2) _____

_____

_____

3) _____

_____

_____

4) _____

_____

_____

5) _____

_____

_____

NOTES:

DAY 21

Express 5 Gratitude thoughts for useful or favorite clothes and accessories. (I am grateful for the kneepads that I use to cushion my knees in my magazine merchandising work.)

1) _____

_____

_____

2) _____

_____

_____

3) _____

_____

_____

4) _____

_____

_____

5) _____

_____

_____

NOTES:

DAY 22

Express 5 Gratitude thoughts for the gifts of nature (Rain/sun/wind, etc.)

1) _____

_____

_____

2) _____

_____

_____

3) _____

_____

_____

4) _____

_____

_____

5) _____

_____

_____

NOTES:

DAY 23

Express 5 Gratitude thoughts for accomplishments (personal or at work).

1) _____

_____

_____

2) _____

_____

_____

3) _____

_____

_____

4) _____

_____

_____

5) _____

_____

_____

NOTES:

DAY 24

Express 5 Gratitude thoughts for all workers (teachers, custodians, radiologists, farmers, lawyers, customer service, trucker drivers, computer technicians, etc).

1) _____

_____

_____

2) _____

_____

_____

3) _____

_____

_____

4) _____

_____

_____

5) _____

_____

_____

NOTES:

DAY 25

Express 5 Gratitude thoughts for first responders in emergencies (police, fire fighters, CERT, emergency medical technicians, military, coast guard etc).

1) _____

_____

_____

2) _____

_____

_____

3) _____

_____

_____

4) _____

_____

_____

5) _____

_____

_____

NOTES:

DAY 26

Express 5 Gratitude thoughts for volunteers and volunteering.

1) _____

_____

_____

2) _____

_____

_____

3) _____

_____

_____

4) _____

_____

_____

5) _____

_____

_____

NOTES:

DAY 27

Express 5 Gratitude thoughts for positive changes this year compared to last year (better job, lost weight, graduation etc).

1) _____

_____

_____

2) _____

_____

_____

3) _____

_____

_____

4) _____

_____

_____

5) _____

_____

_____

NOTES:

DAY 28

Express 5 Gratitude thoughts for the beauty that exists (children laughing, paintings, and rainbows).

1) _____

_____

_____

2) _____

_____

_____

3) _____

_____

_____

4) _____

_____

_____

5) _____

_____

_____

NOTES:

DAY 29

Express 5 Gratitude thoughts for animals (birds, reptiles, mammals).

1) _____

_____

_____

2) _____

_____

_____

3) _____

_____

_____

4) _____

_____

_____

5) _____

_____

_____

NOTES:

DAY 30

Express 5 Gratitude thoughts for your favorite books or writings in the past.

1) _____

_____

_____

2) _____

_____

_____

3) _____

_____

_____

4) _____

_____

_____

5) _____

_____

_____

NOTES:

DAY 31

Express 5 Gratitude thoughts for your favorite music or TV shows (in the present).

1) _____

_____

_____

2) _____

_____

_____

3) _____

_____

_____

4) _____

_____

_____

5) _____

_____

_____

NOTES:

NOTES/GOALS:

DAY 32

Express 5 Gratitude thoughts for your bodily functions (swallowing, coughing when needed, etc).

1) _____

_____

_____

2) _____

_____

_____

3) _____

_____

_____

4) _____

_____

_____

5) _____

_____

_____

NOTES:

DAY 33

Express 5 Gratitude thoughts for your favorite memories (wedding, prom, reunion).

1) _____

_____

_____

2) _____

_____

_____

3) _____

_____

_____

4) _____

_____

_____

5) _____

_____

_____

NOTES:

DAY 34

Express 5 Gratitude thoughts for devices that make life easier (eye glasses, turn signals, ink pens).

1) _____

_____

_____

2) _____

_____

_____

3) _____

_____

_____

4) _____

_____

_____

5) _____

_____

_____

NOTES:

DAY 35

Express 5 Gratitude thoughts for items that help keep us clean (soap, toothpaste, showers).

1) _____

_____

_____

2) _____

_____

_____

3) _____

_____

_____

4) _____

_____

_____

5) _____

_____

_____

NOTES:

DAY 36

Express 5 Gratitude thoughts for tools (scissors, saws, wrenches).

1) _____

_____

_____

2) _____

_____

_____

3) _____

_____

_____

4) _____

_____

_____

5) _____

_____

_____

NOTES:

DAY 37

Express 5 Gratitude thoughts for eating utensils-items (forks, spoons, plates).

1) _____

_____

_____

2) _____

_____

_____

3) _____

_____

_____

4) _____

_____

_____

5) _____

_____

_____

NOTES:

DAY 38

Express 5 Gratitude thoughts for everything that keeps children safe (car seats, parents, safety locks, safety caps).

1) _____

_____

_____

2) _____

_____

_____

3) _____

_____

_____

4) _____

_____

_____

5) _____

_____

_____

NOTES:

DAY 39

Express 5 Gratitude thoughts for beverages (juice, water, tea, beer).

1) _____

_____

_____

2) _____

_____

_____

3) _____

_____

_____

4) _____

_____

_____

5) _____

_____

_____

NOTES:

DAY 40

Express 5 Gratitude thoughts for courtesy (thank you, pardon me, correctly sneezing into crook of arm).

1) _____

_____

_____

2) _____

_____

_____

3) _____

_____

_____

4) _____

_____

_____

5) _____

_____

_____

NOTES:

DAY 41

Express 5 Gratitude thoughts for finding something that was lost (keys, watch, a friendship).

1) _____

_____

_____

2) _____

_____

_____

3) _____

_____

_____

4) _____

_____

_____

5) _____

_____

_____

NOTES:

DAY 42

Express 5 Gratitude thoughts for awards, licenses, diplomas, or certificates.

1) _____

_____

_____

2) _____

_____

_____

3) _____

_____

_____

4) _____

_____

_____

5) _____

_____

_____

NOTES:

DAY 43

Express 5 Gratitude thoughts for great bargains (coupons, sales, reuse, and bonus points).

1) _____

_____

_____

2) _____

_____

_____

3) _____

_____

_____

4) _____

_____

_____

5) _____

_____

_____

NOTES:

DAY 44

Express 5 Gratitude thoughts for strength of your ancestors (traveling to a new land, overcoming hardships, having no money).

1) _____

_____

_____

2) _____

_____

_____

3) _____

_____

_____

4) _____

_____

_____

5) _____

_____

_____

NOTES:

DAY 45

Express 5 Gratitude thoughts for holidays or weekends/rest days.

1) _____

_____

_____

2) _____

_____

_____

3) _____

_____

_____

4) _____

_____

_____

5) _____

_____

_____

NOTES:

DAY 46

Express 5 Gratitude thoughts for vacations (staycations/retreats).

1) _____

_____

_____

2) _____

_____

_____

3) _____

_____

_____

4) _____

_____

_____

5) _____

_____

_____

NOTES:

DAY 47

Express 5 Gratitude thoughts for quite time, meditation time, or alone time.

1) _____

_____

_____

2) _____

_____

_____

3) _____

_____

_____

4) _____

_____

_____

5) _____

_____

_____

NOTES:

DAY 48

Express 5 Gratitude thoughts for health practitioners (podiatrists, nurses, dentists).

1) _____

_____

_____

2) _____

_____

_____

3) _____

_____

_____

4) _____

_____

_____

5) _____

_____

_____

NOTES:

DAY 49

Express 5 Gratitude thoughts for your family members who have made their transition (passed away).

1) _____

_____

_____

2) _____

_____

_____

3) _____

_____

_____

4) _____

_____

_____

5) _____

_____

_____

NOTES:

DAY 50

Express 5 Gratitude thoughts for friends in the afterlife (who have made their transition).

1) _____

_____

_____

2) _____

_____

_____

3) _____

_____

_____

4) _____

_____

_____

5) _____

_____

_____

NOTES:

DAY 51

Express 5 Gratitude thoughts for plants/trees/grass.

1) _____

_____

_____

2) _____

_____

_____

3) _____

_____

_____

4) _____

_____

_____

5) _____

_____

_____

NOTES:

DAY 52

Express 5 Gratitude thoughts for medicine and/or vitamins.

1) _____

_____

_____

2) _____

_____

_____

3) _____

_____

_____

4) _____

_____

_____

5) _____

_____

_____

NOTES:

DAY 53

Express 5 Gratitude thoughts for types of great weather (snow for skiing, sunshine for weddings, rain for irrigating plants, etc).

1) _____

_____

_____

2) _____

_____

_____

3) _____

_____

_____

4) _____

_____

_____

5) _____

_____

_____

NOTES:

DAY 54

Express 5 Gratitude thoughts for favorite types of vegetables (beets, organic greens for salads, green peppers).

1) _____

_____

_____

2) _____

_____

_____

3) _____

_____

_____

4) _____

_____

_____

5) _____

_____

_____

NOTES:

DAY 55

Express 5 Gratitude thoughts for living arrangements (friends let you use their couch, roommates at a dorm, a first apartment).

1) _____

_____

_____

2) _____

_____

_____

3) _____

_____

_____

4) _____

_____

_____

5) _____

_____

_____

NOTES:

DAY 56

Express 5 Gratitude thoughts for favorite music or TV shows in the past.

1) _____

_____

_____

2) _____

_____

_____

3) _____

_____

_____

4) _____

_____

_____

5) _____

_____

_____

NOTES:

DAY 57

Express 5 Gratitude thoughts for gratitude quotes.

1) _____

_____

_____

2) _____

_____

_____

3) _____

_____

_____

4) _____

_____

_____

5) _____

_____

_____

NOTES:

DAY 58

Express 5 Gratitude thoughts for favorite classes and/or learning experiences in or out of the classroom.

1) _____

_____

_____

2) _____

_____

_____

3) _____

_____

_____

4) _____

_____

_____

5) _____

_____

_____

NOTES:

DAY 59

Express 5 Gratitude thoughts for favorite desserts (hot fudge ice cream puff, apple pie, etc).

1) _____

_____

_____

2) _____

_____

_____

3) _____

_____

_____

4) _____

_____

_____

5) _____

_____

_____

NOTES:

DAY 60

Express 5 Gratitude thoughts for favorite teachers (in and out of the classroom).

1) _____

_____

_____

2) _____

_____

_____

3) _____

_____

_____

4) _____

_____

_____

5) _____

_____

_____

NOTES:

DAY 61

Express 5 Gratitude thoughts for favorite charities or organizations.

1) _____

_____

_____

2) _____

_____

_____

3) _____

_____

_____

4) _____

_____

_____

5) _____

_____

_____

NOTES:

DAY 62

Express 5 Gratitude thoughts for prayers, meditations, or reflections.

1) _____

_____

_____

2) _____

_____

_____

3) _____

_____

_____

4) _____

_____

_____

5) _____

_____

_____

NOTES:

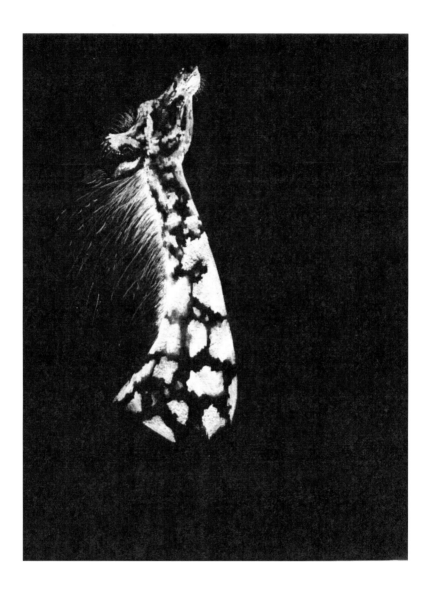

NOTES/GOALS:

DAY 63

Express 5 Gratitude thoughts for today's activities (getting up this morning, ability to think, ability to write, ability to read).

1) _____

_____

_____

2) _____

_____

_____

3) _____

_____

_____

4) _____

_____

_____

5) _____

_____

_____

NOTES:

DAY 64

Express 5 Gratitude thoughts for favorite poem, reading or verse.

1) _____

_____

_____

2) _____

_____

_____

3) _____

_____

_____

4) _____

_____

_____

5) _____

_____

_____

NOTES:

DAY 65

Express 5 Gratitude thoughts for relationships (relatives, work, romantic).

1) _____

_____

_____

2) _____

_____

_____

3) _____

_____

_____

4) _____

_____

_____

5) _____

_____

_____

NOTES:

DAY 66

Express 5 Gratitude thoughts for stores (Neighborhood Mom and Pop, Costco, Target, Sears, Spartans, CVS, etc).

1) _____

_____

_____

2) _____

_____

_____

3) _____

_____

_____

4) _____

_____

_____

5) _____

_____

_____

NOTES:

DAY 67

Express 5 Gratitude thoughts for kept resolutions (lost weight, gave up candy, volunteered, went back to school etc).

1) _____

_____

_____

2) _____

_____

_____

3) _____

_____

_____

4) _____

_____

_____

5) _____

_____

_____

NOTES:

DAY 68

Express 5 Gratitude thoughts for restaurants or potluck.

1) _____

_____

_____

2) _____

_____

_____

3) _____

_____

_____

4) _____

_____

_____

5) _____

_____

_____

NOTES:

DAY 69

Express 5 Gratitude thoughts for home made meals past or present.

1) _____

_____

_____

2) _____

_____

_____

3) _____

_____

_____

4) _____

_____

_____

5) _____

_____

_____

NOTES:

DAY 70

Express 5 Gratitude thoughts for devices that clean (brooms, mops, rags).

1) _____

_____

_____

2) _____

_____

_____

3) _____

_____

_____

4) _____

_____

_____

5) _____

_____

_____

NOTES:

DAY 71

Express 5 Gratitude thoughts for devices to help in floor transition (escalators, elevators, steps).

1) _____

_____

_____

2) _____

_____

_____

3) _____

_____

_____

4) _____

_____

_____

5) _____

_____

_____

NOTES:

DAY 72

Express 5 Gratitude thoughts for devices to help when physically needed (crutches, wheelchair, casts, and canes).

1) _____

_____

_____

2) _____

_____

_____

3) _____

_____

_____

4) _____

_____

_____

5) _____

_____

_____

NOTES:

DAY 73

Express 5 Gratitude thoughts for actors and/or athletes.

1) _____

_____

_____

2) _____

_____

_____

3) _____

_____

_____

4) _____

_____

_____

5) _____

_____

_____

NOTES:

DAY 74

Express 5 Gratitude thoughts for singers and/or musicians.

1) _____

_____

_____

2) _____

_____

_____

3) _____

_____

_____

4) _____

_____

_____

5) _____

_____

_____

NOTES:

DAY 75

Express 5 Gratitude thoughts for dancers and/or comedians.

1) _____

_____

_____

2) _____

_____

_____

3) _____

_____

_____

4) _____

_____

_____

5) _____

_____

_____

NOTES:

DAY 76

Express 5 Gratitude thoughts for times of peace in the world.

1) _____

_____

_____

2) _____

_____

_____

3) _____

_____

_____

4) _____

_____

_____

5) _____

_____

_____

NOTES:

DAY 77

Express 5 Gratitude thoughts for service animals and/or the people and organizations who train the service animals (Seeing Eye dog, drug sniffing dogs, K9 dogs, etc).

1) _____

_____

_____

2) _____

_____

_____

3) _____

_____

_____

4) _____

_____

_____

5) _____

_____

_____

NOTES:

DAY 78

Express 5 Gratitude thoughts for farms and the farmers and farm workers (rural and/or urban).

1) _____

_____

_____

2) _____

_____

_____

3) _____

_____

_____

4) _____

_____

_____

5) _____

_____

_____

NOTES:

DAY 79

Express 5 Gratitude thoughts for great imagination and innovation (inventions and their inventors) past and present (computers, traffic signals, cars, etc).

1) _____

_____

_____

2) _____

_____

_____

3) _____

_____

_____

4) _____

_____

_____

5) _____

_____

_____

NOTES:

DAY 80

Express 5 Gratitude thoughts for exercise (types, the benefits, and your progress).

1) _____

_____

_____

2) _____

_____

_____

3) _____

_____

_____

4) _____

_____

_____

5) _____

_____

_____

NOTES:

DAY 81

Express 5 Gratitude thoughts for patience (from self and from others).

1) _____

_____

_____

2) _____

_____

_____

3) _____

_____

_____

4) _____

_____

_____

5) _____

_____

_____

NOTES:

DAY 82

Express 5 Gratitude thoughts for arriving at your destinations safely (past and present).

1) _____

_____

_____

2) _____

_____

_____

3) _____

_____

_____

4) _____

_____

_____

5) _____

_____

_____

NOTES:

DAY 83

Express 5 Gratitude thoughts for useful technology (robotics, solar panels, and light rail).

1) _____

_____

_____

2) _____

_____

_____

3) _____

_____

_____

4) _____

_____

_____

5) _____

_____

_____

NOTES:

DAY 84

Express 5 Gratitude thoughts for infrastructure (streets, bridges, sewerage piping, etc.).

1) _____

_____

_____

2) _____

_____

_____

3) _____

_____

_____

4) _____

_____

_____

5) _____

_____

_____

NOTES:

DAY 85

Express 5 Gratitude thoughts for storage space (closets, garages, attics, storage lockers).

1) _____

_____

_____

2) _____

_____

_____

3) _____

_____

_____

4) _____

_____

_____

5) _____

_____

_____

NOTES:

__DAY 86__

Express 5 Gratitude thoughts for special men in your life (dad, stepfather, uncles, mentors, father-in-law, etc).

1) _____

_____

_____

2) _____

_____

_____

3) _____

_____

_____

4) _____

_____

_____

5) _____

_____

_____

NOTES:

DAY 87

Express 5 Gratitude thoughts for special women in your life (mom, stepmother, mother-in-law, grandmothers, aunts).

1) _____

_____

_____

2) _____

_____

_____

3) _____

_____

_____

4) _____

_____

_____

5) _____

_____

_____

NOTES:

DAY 88

Express 5 Gratitude thoughts for special children in your life (sons, daughters, nieces, nephews, grandchildren, students).

1) _____

_____

_____

2) _____

_____

_____

3) _____

_____

_____

4) _____

_____

_____

5) _____

_____

_____

NOTES:

DAY 89

Express 5 Gratitude thoughts for paying off a bill, home, loan, or debt.

1) _____

_____

_____

2) _____

_____

_____

3) _____

_____

_____

4) _____

_____

_____

5) _____

_____

_____

NOTES:

DAY 90

Express 5 Gratitude thoughts for good sleep and/or naps.

1) _____

_____

_____

2) _____

_____

_____

3) _____

_____

_____

4) _____

_____

_____

5) _____

_____

_____

NOTES:

NOTES/GOALS:

DAY 91

Express 5 Gratitude thoughts for excellent customer service or retail experiences (The service was fast, the representative was courteous, your issue was resolved etc).

1) _____

_____

_____

2) _____

_____

_____

3) _____

_____

_____

4) _____

_____

_____

5) _____

_____

_____

NOTES:

DAY 92

Express 5 Gratitude thoughts for helpful and/or fun conversations (someone hands you an extra coupon for your product in the store, someone walks you over to a product you could not find, someone kindly whispers that you have tissue stuck to your shoe, someone hands you back a twenty dollar bill that you accidentally dropped).

1) _____

_____

_____

2) _____

_____

_____

3) _____

_____

_____

4) _____

_____

_____

5) _____

_____

_____

NOTES:

DAY 93

Express 5 Gratitude thoughts for joyful sights and/or sounds (birds singing, babies laughing, kittens and puppies on a U-tube video).

1) _____

_____

_____

2) _____

_____

_____

3) _____

_____

_____

4) _____

_____

_____

5) _____

_____

_____

NOTES:

Congratulations!!!!

You should be VERY proud of your accomplishment. You have completed one full season of gratitude (90+ days).

This is a habit that deserves to be continued. I am sure that this gratitude perspective has made changes in your quality of life.

Has there been any positive change in your health and healing, your financial prosperity, your emotional prosperity, or your relationships?

Please let us know on Facebook at: seasonofgratitudeThomas-Bass.
We look forward to hearing from you.